KOLAH
THE KOALA

Words by Jon Resnick

Design by Jan Davis

Photography by George Apostolidis,
Jan Davis and Jon Resnick

TRUE-TO-LIFE BOOKS

Educating children about endangered species

A great big koala hug to the Apostolidis family -
George for his time and talent, and Cathy,
Anastasia, Christina and Alexandra for their
friendship and hospitality.

UNEP

Supported by the United Nations
Environment Programme

Special thanks to Greg Parker of Ballarat
Wildlife and Reptile Park, Stephen Meehan
of the Koala Conservation Centre, and Bruce
Kubbere of Featherdale Wildlife Park. The
photographs you see would not have been
possible without the generosity of C.P.L.
Services of Melbourne. Many thanks.

Printed by Hong Kong Prime Printing Co. Ltd.
Colour Separations by Karl's Graphics Services Ltd.

Hi, my name is Kolah and I'm a koala.
I live in Australia where my ancestors
have lived for over 15 million years.

My home is in the Eucalyptus trees,
which are necessary for my survival.
They give me shade, comfortable
branches to curl up on and,
most important, leaves to eat.

Some people think koalas are bears, but that's not true at all. We are marsupials, a primitive mammal with a pouch for our young, similar to kangaroos, wombats and possums.

Meet Cuddles, my baby sister.
She's ten months old.

Generally, koalas prefer to live alone.
My mother will look after Cuddles until
she's about one. Then they will separate.
At the age of around two, Cuddles will start
her own family. But for now she enjoys
riding on my Mum's back - what fun!

My father is nearly twice the size of my mother and weighs about 12 kilos. He marks his territory with a smell by using the dark scent gland on his chest. Also he tilts his head back and makes loud "snore-belches" to let others know where he is.

When it comes to food, koalas are not as fussy as people think. We eat the leaves and buds of over 120 varieties of Eucalyptus trees.

Occasionally we feed on several other trees, like the olden wattle, coast tea-tree and cherry tree. Our total diet s only 500 grams a day, which is equal to a bowl of cereal.

Koalas spend about 19 hours each day
just sleeping and resting.

The reason we don't have much energy is because
we eat so little. It has nothing to do with the chemicals
in the Eucalyptus leaves, which is just a myth.

In fact, we do lots of other things besides sleep, such as

climbing…

grooming…

walking from tree to tree…

…and even jumping from tree to tree.

If you come to visit, you can get a close look at my…

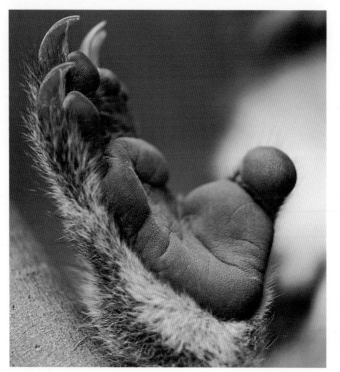

powerful hands and feet…

cute little nose…

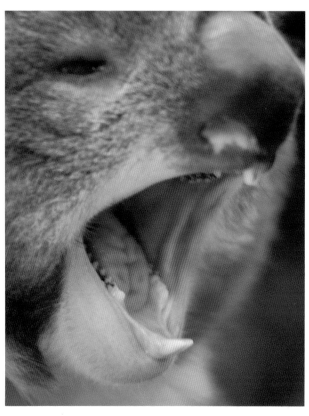

sharp front teeth…

almond-shaped eyes…

…and fluffy ears.

Koalas can live to be around 15 years old.
There are about 400,000 of us left in Australia,
but every day our habitat is being destroyed.

Other dangers include bushfires, drought, starvation
and disease. And in the city areas we are victims of
dogs and cars. We need help if we are to survive.
I hope you care about us because only you can
make a difference.

Thank you for your interest in protecting the koalas. If you would like to help, please support the following organisations and wildlife parks:

AUSTRALIAN KOALA FOUNDATION
G.P.O. Box 9899
Brisbane QLD 4001

THE AUSTRALIAN WILDLIFE FUND
P.O.Box 214
Lindfield NSW 2070

AUSTRALIAN NATURE
CONSERVATION AGENCY
Endangered Species Unit
G.P.O. Box 636
Canberra ACT 2601

THE KOALA PRESERVATION
SOCIETY OF QUEENSLAND
P.O. Box 418
Cleveland QLD 4163

THE KOALA PRESERVATION
SOCIETY OF NEW SOUTH WALES
P.O. Box 236
Port Macquarie NSW 2444

WWF AUSTRALIA
Level 10, 8-10 Bridge Street
G.P.O Box 528
Sydney NSW 2001

BALLARAT WILDLIFE AND
REPTILE PARK
Cnr. Fussell & York Sts.
P.O. Box 1200, Mail Centre
Ballarat VIC 3354

KOALA CONSERVATION CENTRE
Phillip Island Road
Cowes VIC 3922

FEATHERDALE WILDLIFE PARK
217 Kildare Road
Duneside NSW 2767

HEALESVILLE SANCTUARY
Badger Creek Road
Healesville VIC 3777

LONE PINE KOALA SANCTUARY
Jesmond Road
Fig Tree Pocket QLD 4069

FRIENDS OF THE KOALAS INC.
P.O. Box 231
Cowes VIC 3922

MACLEAY KOALA PRESERVATION GROUP
P.O. Box 147
Kempsey NSW

NATIVE ANIMAL TRUST FUND
P.O. Box 544
Raymond Terrace NSW 2324

QUEENSLAND WILDLIFE HOSPITAL
P.O. Box 200
Deception Bay QLD 4508

WILDLIFE CARE NETWORK
P.O. Box 19
Berwick VIC 3806

WIRES TAMWORTH
14 Bourne Street
Tamworth NSW 2340